Pick a Plate

SNACKS

by Charis Mather

Minneapolis, Minnesota

Credits

All images are courtesy of Shutterstock.com, unless otherwise specified. With thanks to Getty Images, Thinkstock Photo, and iStockphoto. Front Cover – ankudi, Poi NATTHAYA, VectorKid, Andrii Symonenko, GoodStudio, NotionPic, Ekaterina_Mikhaylova, SvtM. Background – ankudi. 3 – Tomas Jasinskis, logistock, EkaterinaP, Shapovalova Polina. 6–9 – Designation, 21kompot, KutuzovaDesign, mayalis, Ramcreative, SeekandFind, Katy Flaty, Sudowoodo, Akane1988, Dernkadel, Designation, Dustick, GoodStudio, Pretty Vectors, SThom, Viktoria Sokolova. 10&11 – Top Vector Studio, Neliakott. 12&13 – logistock, Sudowoodo, Neliakott. 14–17 – EkaterinaP, unununij, curiosity. 18–21 – Geraskevich, kaisorn, MariVolkoff, Nadya_Art, Shapovalova Polina. 22&23 – Top Vector Studio, Neliakott, logistock, EkaterinaP, An_Star, unununij, curiosity, Geraskevich, MariVolkoff, Nadya_Art, Shapovalova Polina.

Library of Congress Cataloging-in-Publication Data is available at www.loc.gov or upon request from the publisher.

ISBN: 979-8-88509-349-1 (hardcover)
ISBN: 979-8-88509-471-9 (paperback)
ISBN: 979-8-88509-586-0 (ebook)

© 2023 Booklife Publishing
This edition is published by arrangement with Booklife Publishing.

North American adaptations © 2023 Bearport Publishing Company. All rights reserved. No part of this publication may be reproduced in whole or in part, stored in any retrieval system, or transmitted in any form or by any means, electronic, mechanical, photocopying, recording, or otherwise, without written permission from the publisher.

For more information, write to Bearport Publishing, 5357 Penn Avenue South, Minneapolis, MN 55419.

CONTENTS

What Is in Your Snack? 4

Food Groups: So Much to Choose! 6

Some of Everything 8

Potato Chips OR Popcorn? 10

Yogurt and Fruit OR Frozen Treat? 14

Mini Sausages OR Hummus Plate? 18

Food for Thought 22

Glossary 24

Index 24

WHAT IS IN YOUR SNACK?

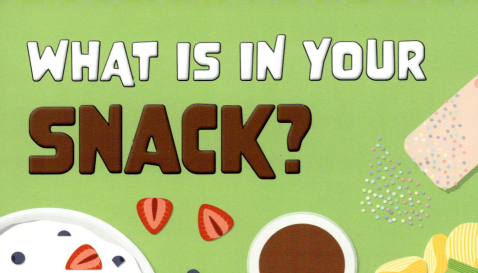

What do you want to eat for a snack? Do you like crackers, fruit, or chips? What about popcorn or carrot sticks? Snacks are a way for us to get **energy** between meals.

Our bodies get energy from the food we eat. Different kinds of food help our bodies in different ways. Eating many different foods helps us stay strong and **healthy**.

FOOD GROUPS
SO MUCH TO CHOOSE!

There are five main groups of food.

Fruits
Foods in this group can be fresh, frozen, or from a can. Eat fruits of many different colors.

Vegetables
These parts of plants help keep us healthy in many ways. It's good to have different kinds on your plate.

Grains

This group has rice, wheat, and other plant seeds. It also has all the foods made from grains, such as bread and pasta.

Protein

Fish, meat, chicken, eggs, peas, nuts, and beans all have protein.

Dairy

This group has milk, cheese, and yogurt. It also includes soy milk and soy yogurt.

SOME OF EVERYTHING

Fruits

Every day, your body needs food from all five groups. This plate shows a **balanced** meal. It can help you have the right kinds of food in the right amounts. Aim to have this balance during your day.

Vegetables

It's okay to eat foods from different groups at different meals.

We should eat veggies, fruits, and grains the most. Foods that have a lot of fat or added sugar can be bad for our bodies. Try to skip them.

Can you pick the plates that have a good balance of food groups?

POTATO CHIPS

Chips are made from potatoes that are thinly sliced and then **fried** in oil. Oil is a kind of fat. Eating too much fat can be bad for your body.

OR POPCORN?

Popcorn is a whole grain. It has a lot of **fiber**, which is good for your heart and tummy. But if you add butter, this snack can have a lot of fat, too.

Which **plate** would **you** pick?

Which plate did you pick? The popcorn plate has a healthy whole grain. Still, both snacks can have lots of fat from oil or butter. Let's make both plates better!

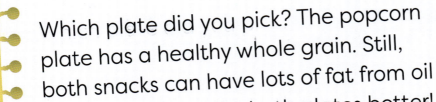

Instead of potato chips, try a crunchy seaweed snack.

Eat some healthy veggies with your chips.

For some protein, add nuts to a popcorn snack mix.

Use only a little bit of butter and salt.

YOGURT AND FRUIT

Yogurt is in the dairy food group. Dairy foods have **calcium**, which keeps our bones and teeth strong. Adding fruit to the snack gives us even more healthy **nutrients**.

OR FROZEN TREAT?

Frozen treats can have dairy and fruit, too. But they often have a lot of sugar. Eating too much sugar is not healthy.

Which **plate** would **you** pick?

Which plate did you pick? Mixing dairy and fruit is a good balance. Let's just try to cut down on extra sugar. How can we make both snacks better?

Add nuts for some protein.

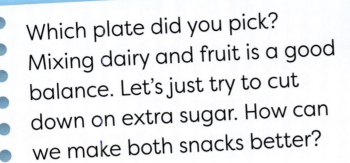

Try different kinds of fruit.

Each kind of fruit has its own mix of nutrients to help our bodies in different ways.

Make healthy treats at home by freezing fresh fruit.

Try mixing fruits in a blender with yogurt for a smoothie!

Frozen watermelon slices can be yummy treats.

MINI SAUSAGES

Sausages are made from meat and are full of protein. Our bodies need protein to **heal** and grow. But sausages also have a lot of fat.

OR HUMMUS PLATE?

Hummus is a dip made from a kind of bean. It also has a lot of protein. You can dip healthy veggies and crackers into hummus.

Which **plate** would **you** pick?

Which plate did you pick? The mini sausages have more fat and protein than we need in a snack. The hummus plate has a good balance. Still, we can make both snacks better!

Pick sausage with less fat, such as turkey sausage.

Add foods from other groups to your sausage plate, too.

For some dairy, drink a glass of milk with your snack.

Choose whole grain crackers to eat with your hummus.

FOOD FOR THOUGHT

Now, you know more about balanced meals. Can you choose your own healthy snack? Remember to pick foods from different groups.

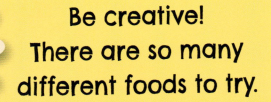

Be creative! There are so many different foods to try.

GLOSSARY

balanced the right amount of things

calcium something in food that is good for bones and teeth

energy the power to be able to do things

fiber something in food that helps a person's tummy stay healthy

fried cooked in hot oil

heal to become healthy again

healthy when the body is working well and is not sick

nutrients things in food that people need to grow and be healthy

INDEX

dairy 7, 9, 14, 21, 23
fat 9–12, 18, 20
fiber 11
fruit 4, 6, 8–9, 14, 16–17, 20, 23
grains 7, 9, 11–12, 21, 23
protein 7, 9, 13, 16, 18–20, 23
sugar 9, 15–16
vegetables 6, 8–9, 12, 19, 23